D1370656

Everyday Prayers for Children

EVERYDAY
PRAYERS
for
Children

DIMENSIONS
FOR LIVING

NASHVILLE

EVERYDAY PRAYERS FOR CHILDREN

Copyright © 1993 by Dimensions for Living

This book is printed on recycled, acid-free paper.

Scripture quotations, unless otherwise noted, are taken
from the New Revised Standard Version Bible, Copyright
© 1989 by The National Council of The Churches of
Christ in the U.S.A. Used by permission.

Scripture quotations marked KJV are from the King James
Version of the Bible.

95 96 97 98 99 00 01 02 — 10 9 8 7 6 5 4

MANUFACTURED IN THE UNITED STATES OF AMERICA

Contents

For Adults

It is certainly more important to teach a child to pray than to say prayers, but some of us cannot be as original and creative in our prayer life as others. We need forms that will express the content of our thought and feeling. Many of the prayers in this book are expressions of devotion that have gained value by centuries of use. Others are newly written. You will find simple and appropriate forms of prayer to use with your children in their efforts to talk with God.

Encourage your child to pray spontaneously, even when the efforts seem grotesque and humorous to you. The more natural this conversation between your child and God, the better. Set aside a time each day to pray with your child. Your quiet companionship during this time will make it a period of anticipation and delight.

For Children

Praying is just like talking to your friends or your parents. Think about the times you have been happy and excited. Don't you want to tell someone about your feelings? How about when you are sad or afraid? Other times you may be feeling sorry because you have done something wrong and want to ask forgiveness. God is always there to listen.

These prayers are some of the ways other people have thought about God and talked to God. They will help you get started when you want to pray.

Jesus knew how to pray better than anyone. When his friends asked him to tell them how, he gave them what we today call the Lord's Prayer. He reminded them that we are all members of God's family. God loves us and knows what is best for us. When we pray, we should always praise and thank God for caring for us. We should ask God's help in making the world a good place to live. When we have been unkind or selfish or when we have disobeyed our parents or teachers, we can talk to God. We can tell God how sorry we are just as we tell our parents or friends. God will forgive us just as other people do.

After you have used the prayers in this book for a while you may find that you want to talk to God in your own words. You may want to write down your own prayers and thoughts about God. You can even make your own book of prayers.

The Lord's Prayer

Our father, who art in heaven,
hallowed be thy name.
Thy Kingdom come,
Thy will be done
on earth as it is in heaven.
Give us this day our daily bread.
And forgive us our trespasses,
as we forgive those who trespass
    against us.
And lead us not into temptation,
but deliver us from evil.
For thine is the kingdom,
and the power, and the glory,
forever. Amen.

To Be
Said Before Praying

Before my words of prayer are said,
I'll close my eyes and bow my head,
That I may think to whom I pray,
That I may mean the words I say.

To say my prayers is not to pray
Unless I mean the words I say,
Unless I think to whom I speak
And with my heart his favor seek.

Then let me when I come to pray
Not only mind the words I say,
But let me try with earnest care
To have my heart go with my prayer.

Motion Prayer

We fold our hands that we may be
From earthly play and work set free;
We bow our heads as we draw near
The King of kings, our Father dear;
We close our eyes, that we may see
Nothing to take our thoughts from thee.
Into our hearts we pray you will come,
And may they each become your home;
This is our prayer we bring to thee.
Then open our eyes, your light to see,
Lift up our heads to praise you still,
Open our hands to do your will.

Gentle Jesus, Meek and Mild

Gentle Jesus, meek and mild,
Look upon a little child;
Pity my simplicity,
Suffer me to come to Thee.

Fain I would to Thee be brought;
Dearest God, forbid it not;
Give me, dearest God, a place
In the kingdom of Thy grace.

Put Thy hands upon my head,
Let me in Thine arms be stayed;
Let me lean upon Thy breast,
Lull, lull me, Lord, to rest.

Hold me fast in Thy embrace,
Let me see Thy smiling face.
Give me, Lord, Thy blessing give;
Pray for me, and I shall live.

Lamb of God, I look to Thee;
Thou shalt my Example be;
Thou are gentle, meek and mild,
Thou wast once a little Child.

Fain I would be as Thou art;
Give me Thy obedient heart.
Thou art pitiful and kind;
Let me have Thy loving mind.

Let me above all fulfill
God my heavenly Father's will;
Never His good Spirit grieve,
Only to His glory live.

Thou didst live to God alone,
Thou didst never seek Thine own;
Thou Thyself didst never please.
God was all Thy happiness.

Loving Jesu, gentle Lamb,
In Thy gracious hands I am,
Make me, Savior, what Thou art,
Live Thyself within my heart.

Charles Wesley

Now the Day Is Over

Now the day is over,
Night is drawing nigh,
Shadows of the evening
Steal across the sky;

Jesus, give the weary
Calm and sweet repose;
With thy tendrest blessing
May our eyelids close.

Grant to little children
Visions bright of thee;
Guard the Sailors tossing
On the deep blue sea.

Comfort every sufferer
Watching late in pain;
Those who plan some evil
From their sins restrain.

Through the long night watches,
May thine angels spread
Their white wings above me,
Watching round my bed.

When the morning wakens,
Then may I arise
Pure and fresh and sinless
In thy holy eyes.

Sabin Baring-Gould

Jesus,
Tender Shepherd

Jesus, tender Shepherd hear me;
Bless thy little lamb tonight;
Through the darkness be thou near me,
Keep me safe till morning light.

All this day thy hand has led me,
And I thank thee for thy care;
Thou has warmed me, clothed and fed me;
Listen to my evening prayer!

Let my sins be all forgiven;
Bless the friends I love so well:
Take us all at last to heaven,
Happy there with thee to dwell.

Mary Duncan

For the
Beauty of the Earth

For the beauty of the earth,
   For the glory of the skies,
For the love which from our birth
   Over and around us lies,
Lord of all, to Thee we raise
This our hymn of grateful praise.

For the joy of human love,
   Brother, sister, parent, child,
Friends on earth and friends above,
   For all gentle thoughts and mild,
Lord of all, to Thee we raise
This our hymn of grateful praise.

Folliott S. Pierpoint

At Evening

Day is dying in the west,
Heav'n is touching earth with rest;
Wait and worship while the night
Sets her evening lamps alight
   Through all the sky.

Lord of life, beneath the dome
Of the universe, Thy home,
Gather us, who seek Thy face,
To the fold of Thy embrace,
   For Thou art nigh.

Holy, Holy, Holy, Lord God of Hosts!
Heav'n and earth are full of Thee!
Heav'n and earth are praising Thee,
   O Lord most high!

For Children Everywhere

Lord, teach me to love your children
    everywhere, because
You are their father and mine.
AMEN.

Lord, I ask your help in learning how to
pray. Teach me how to put my whole self
into my prayers. Help my words have
meaning, so that my thoughts reach you.
Be near to me every hour of every day.
This is always my prayer. AMEN.

Let the words of my mouth
    and the meditation of my heart
be acceptable in thy sight,
O Lord, my rock and my redeemer.

Psalm 19:14

We give Thee but Thine own,
Whate'er the gift may be:
All that we have is Thine alone,
A trust, O Lord, from Thee.

William Walsham How

Breathe on me, Breath of God,
Fill me with life anew,
That I may love what thou dost love,
And do what thou wouldst do.

Edwin Hatch

God bless all those that I love;
God bless all those that love me;
God bless all those that love those that
    I love,
And all those that love those that love
    me.

From an old *New England Sampler*

O Holy Jesus,
Most merciful Redeemer,
Friend and Brother,
May I know Thee more clearly,
Love Thee more dearly,
And follow Thee more nearly. AMEN.

Richard of Chichester

God be in my head,
And in my understanding;
God be in mine eyes,
And in my looking;
God be in my mouth
And in my speaking;
God be in my heart,
And in my thinking;
God be at my end and at my departing.

Sarum Primer

Christ as a Light, illumine and guide me,
Christ as a Shield o'ershadow and cover
   me.
Christ be under me,
Christ be over me,
Christ be beside me on left hand and on
   right.
Christ before me, behind me, about me,
Christ this day be within and without
   me. AMEN.

St. Patrick

O Lord, I am happy because you love me, and I pray that I may never forget how much it pleases you when I am happy and good and useful. AMEN.

Heavenly Father, help me keep my temper just this minute. AMEN.

For the Fun of Singing

It's such fun to sing a song,
To sing the music sweet and long;
While we go about our play
It keeps us happy all the day!
Because you put these happy songs
Within our hearts where joy belongs
We thank you, loving Lord! Amen.

Arletta Christman Harvey

When It Rains

Dear God,
I'm speaking for the grass and flowers,
The hills and trees that need the showers;
For though I can't go out to play,
The whole earth loves this rainy day!
Thank you, God. For them, I say,
Thank you for the rain today! Amen.

Arletta Christman Harvey

An Easter Prayer

I sing this happy prayer, Dear God,
For joy and Easter-time,
For birds that sing
And earth so fair,
for springtime beauty everywhere!

And I know why—for Jesus lives!
In all the world today
It's "waking time."
And glad hearts say,
"We thank You, God, for Easter Day!"

Arletta Christman Harvey

For My Mother

Dear God, I love my mother,
But, I find it hard to say
The words that tell my love for her
Upon this Mother's Day.

If I'm afraid or I get hurt
She hears me when I call;
She loves me so, and understands
My problems—one and all!

Oh, thank you God, for all she does,
Her love and care for me;
Please tell her heart the lovely things
I whisper now, to thee. Amen.

Arletta Christman Harvey

When We're Happy at Our Play

Dear God, because you're everywhere,
We do not always kneel to pray;
You hear our words of thankfulness
While we are at our play!

You know the gladness in our hearts;
You love to see us work and play;
And you will watch o'er all we do
Throughout each happy day!

Thank you, dear God, for happiness,
And while we play, be near to bless.

Arletta Christman Harvey

I'm Glad for My Friends

Dear God,
It would be very lonely here,
Without our friends,
To run and play
The whole long day!

I'm glad you made the world this way,
Where girls and boys
Can share their fun
With everyone!

Please help me to be kind and fair
To all my friends—this is my prayer.

Arletta Christman Harvey

For Vacation Days

There's a happy sort of feeling, God,
That seems to come always
When school is closed and summertime
Brings back vacation days!
I'm sure you know just what I mean—
We're free to run and play,
To swim and go on picnics,
Or to fish the whole long day!
O thank you, God, for the ways
Of happy, free, vacation days!

Arletta Christman Harvey

For Sunshine and Flowers

For sunshine warm and kind,
For flowers that I find
Out in my yard,
For pretty stones and birds that sing,
For soft, green grass and everything,
Father, I thank you.

Arletta Christman Harvey

Thanks for My Dog

Dear God, I think you know
How little dogs can grow
Into the hearts of girls and boys.

He begs for me to play,
And knows each word I say,
I love his barks and noise!

Please bless my dog, dear Lord, I pray,
And keep him safe, for me, always!

Arletta Christman Harvey

For Picnic Days

These days seem meant for picnics, God,
The whispering breeze
Among the trees,
Warm sunshine bright and fair,
The stars at night,
The campfire's light,
What happiness is there!
So with our friends, we pause to praise,
To thank you for these picnic days. Amen.

Arletta Christman Harvey

For School Days

Each Morning as I start to school
Dear Lord, in thankfulness I pray:

For this day of new beginnings,
For my friends, our fun and play,
For the teachers as they guide me
In the learning of this day.

For thy care that guards me always,
For the love that holds me true;
Keep me now, dear Heavenly Lord,
At my best the whole day through. Amen.

Arletta Christman Harvey

For the Game

Thank you, dear God, for the game
Where each of us must do our best,
Where none of us can play alone
But must always depend on the rest.

Help me then, God, in this game
That I shall not fail at my part;
Keep me honest and strong, ever true
to the things I count right in my heart.
Amen.

Arletta Christman Harvey

Thanks for My Kitty

Dear Lord,
I thank you for my little pet,
This kitty, soft and warm,
She seems to feel so very sure
I'll keep her safe from harm.

And I feel just the same, Dear Lord,
That you care, too, you see;
So I'll be kind and good to her,
While you are loving me! Amen.

At Bedtime

Dear God, I love the friendly night,
The stars and quiet sky,
And as I kneel beside my bed
I feel your love close by.

For all this happy day has brought,
For all my loved ones near,
For friends and pets and happiness,
I thank you, Savior dear.

Bless little children everywhere
And keep us in your loving care. Amen.

Arletta Christman Harvey

Prayers of Thanksgiving and Praise

Dear God, we thank you for everything good in our lives. We pray that our hearts will always respond to your goodness and that we will grow to be more like you. We pray in the spirit of Christ. AMEN.

Loving Lord, we have learned that we do not need to make out lists of any kind for you because you already know our needs and our wishes. Help us always to be close to you as you are close to us. We know that every good thing comes from you without our asking when our hearts are right and our spirits are ready to receive. For all this we give you our thanks. AMEN.

Everlasting Lord, thank you for the kindness of your love that you show to me
every day in many, many ways. Help me to
be as kind to other people as you are to
me. I know that you are with me every
hour of every day. Thank you for all things.
AMEN.

Lord Jesus, even though you lived long ago you are a close friend to me today. I believe in your way of life and want with all my heart to follow you. I believe your promise that you will always be with me. Thank you for showing me the Father, who gives me all good things. AMEN.

Dear God, I feel and know your love.
Thank you for this gift. AMEN.

I am thankful, Lord, for my home and for
those who love me. Thank you for watching over me each day. Thank you for your
love that never ends. AMEN.

Dear Father, I am thankful for the bright sky, for my food, for the fresh air to breathe and for clean, clear water to drink. Thank you for all the good things in my life. AMEN.

Thank you, Father in heaven, for all my blessings. Thank you for a good land that grows good food. Help me to appreciate all that I have and to share it with others. AMEN.

Thank you, Lord, for my friends and neighbors. Thank you for my country that is filled with friendly neighbors. Help me to think kindly of all people everywhere. AMEN.

Thank you, God, for little things and for big things. Thank you for love. Help our family to be happy together. Bless all families everywhere. AMEN.

Dear heavenly Father, bless everyone in this house. Bless all our neighbors, all our friends, all our relatives. Thank you for your goodness to us. We pray that we will always be good to each other and to all we meet. In Jesus' name. AMEN.

O God, I want to say thank you for the opportunity of learning. Help me to keep my eyes, ears, and heart open to see, to hear, and to receive. AMEN.

God bless little children today everywhere on earth. Bless the children who are hungry, who have no home and who need someone to love them. Bless the children who have too little and those who have too much. AMEN.

Loving God, thank you for the lights of heaven—the sun, the moon, the stars. Thank you for the beauty of the day and the night. Thank you for sending Jesus to be the light of the world. AMEN.

Dear Lord, I pray that today I will have a cheerful heart to match the beauty of the day. Help me to be unselfish and kind to everyone I meet. Make all my thoughts good thoughts. Fill me with your love. AMEN.

Dear heavenly Father, thank you for my home and for my family. Help our family to work together to make our home strong and filled with laughter and love. AMEN.

Dear God, thank you for your love. I see it all around me and I feel it inside myself. I want to love as you do, so that I can make the world around me a better place. Help me to live like Jesus. In his name I pray. AMEN.

Dear Lord, I need your loving care. Help me to always think good thoughts and to do good deeds. AMEN.

O heavenly Father, thank you for the good and beautiful world that you gave us. Give us healthy bodies and clean minds. Teach us how to keep them that way by the wise use of your gifts. In Jesus' name. AMEN.

Thank you, Almighty Giver, for the earth that grows our food. Thank you for the workers who plant and tend and harvest and distribute it. Thank you for the life in every seed and cell.

Thank you for your life in every living thing. AMEN.

Dear Father, show me the right way to live. Show me how to make this day a good day for myself and for everyone I meet. I cannot hear your voice or see your guiding hand with physical ears or eyes, but I know you are near to me. I will put my trust in you. AMEN.

Father of Life, thank you for my life and all it offers. Help me to find opportunities to help other people. Thank you for my mind. Help me to use it well and to think often of you. Forgive me when I am selfish and stubborn. Help me to grow more like Jesus. In his name. AMEN.

Dear Lord, thank you for always being with me. Thank you for all your gifts. Show me how to use your gifts to make a difference in the world. AMEN.

Dear God, you are giving us blessings all the time: help us to be a blessing.

You gave us our hands: help us to use them to work for you.

You gave us our feet: send them on your errands.

You gave us our voices: hear them speak only gentleness and truth.

You gave us our mind to think: help us to think only pleasant, kind thoughts.

You have made our lives pleasant every day with love: help us to make other lives happier every day with our love.

Help us to please you, Lord. Help us to learn; some little deed to thank you with, instead of words; some little prayer to do instead of say; some little thing to give you, because you never tire of giving us so much. AMEN.

Prayer in Sickness

Dear heavenly Father, since I am sick, give me patience so that I may bear this illness without complaining. Help all those who love me and are taking care of me. I thank you because I am your child and you are loving me and taking care of me. Make me well and strong again. AMEN.

A Prayer for All Times

The Lord bless us, and keep us.
The Lord make his face to shine upon us,
    and be gracious to us.
The Lord lift up his countenance upon us,
    and give us peace.

Morning Prayers

I thank you, Lord, for you have kept
Me safe and healthy while I slept.
Stay with me, Lord, throughout the day
And lead me in your own good way,
And this in Jesus' name I pray.

Now I wake and see the light;
'Tis God has kept me through the night.
To him I lift my voice and pray
That he will keep me through the day.

New England Primer

I thank thee, Lord, for quiet rest,
    And for thy care of me;
O let me through this day be blest,
    And kept from harm by thee.

O, let me thank thee, kind thou art
    To children such as I,
Give me a gentle, loving heart;
    Be thou my Friend on high.

Beginners' Reading Book

For this new morning with its light,
For rest and shelter of the night,
For health and food, for home and friends
For everything his goodness sends,
We thank the heavenly Father.

Dear Lord, we thank you for your care,
    And all your mercy sends;
For food we eat, for clothes we wear,
    Our health and home and friends.
AMEN.

Now before we work today
Let us not forget to pray
To God who kept us through the night
And woke us with the morning light.
Help us, Lord, to love you more
Than we have ever loved before
In our work and in our play,
Be with us all throughout the day. AMEN.

Table Graces

Be present at our table, Lord;
Be here and everywhere adored.
Thy mercies bless, and grant that we
May feast in fellowship with Thee. Amen.

John Wesley

The Johnny Appleseed Grace

Oh, the Lord is good to me,
And so I thank the Lord
for giving me the things I need:
the sun, the rain, and the appleseed,
Oh, the Lord is good to me.

God is great and God is good,
And we thank Him for our food;
By His hand we must be fed,
Give us, Lord, our daily bread. AMEN.

Come, Lord Jesus, be our guest,
And make the meal Thou givest blest.

Bless us, O Lord, and these Thy gifts,
which we are about to receive from Thy
bounty, through Christ our Lord. Amen.

Bless me, O Lord, and let my food
strengthen me to serve thee,
for Jesus Christ's sake. Amen.

The New England Primer

For these and for all your gifts of love
We give you thanks and praise;
Look down, O Father, from above,
And bless us all our days.

In the middle of our work and play, dear
Savior, we gather around your table. You
have covered it from your kindness and we
praise you for your gifts to us. May this
food give us strength to work for you. We
ask it in your name. AMEN.

Gracious God, as we come to another meal, we pray that we will not be selfish or greedy or careless with the food you have provided for us. Stop us when we are doing wrong things and show us how to do right things. Keep us from saying or thinking any unkind thoughts. Help us to help others, just as you do. In your son's name. AMEN.

Dear God, thank you for our family and our friends and for this food. Help us always to think and live like Jesus, in whose name we pray. AMEN.

Thank you, God, for fruit and vegetables and meat and bread. Thank you for all good things. Thank you for taking care of us even when we are not grateful. Keep on taking care of all the people in the world, we pray, and show us how to do our part to help. AMEN.

Dear God, thank you for each dish of food on this table. Bless all the people who had a part in growing, harvesting, and preparing these good things. AMEN.

Father in heaven, thank you for this food from your good earth. Thank you for our home and our family. Sit with us at the table and guide us in all we think and say and do. Stay with us all through the day. AMEN.

Prayers After Eating

We thank you, dear Lord, for what you have given us to eat and drink. Help us now to leave the table and do all our work for you. We know you love and care for us. AMEN.

Dear Father in heaven, we thank you
    today
For food and for clothing, for work and for
    play.
Now help us all gladly to do what is right.
And bring us in health to our bedtime
tonight. AMEN.

Bedtime Prayers

Four corners has my bed,
Four angels round my head:
Matthew, Mark, Luke, and John,
Bless the bed that I lie on.

Good Night

Good night! Good night!
Far flies the light;
But still God's love
Shall flame above,
Making all bright.
    Good night! Good night!

Attributed to Victor Hugo

Now I lay me down to sleep
I pray Thee, Lord, my soul to keep,
In peace and safety 'till I wake,
And this I ask for Jesus' sake.

Now I lay me down to sleep.
I pray the Lord my soul to keep
While I live I want to be
From quick and angry thoughts set free.
With gentle thoughts and smiling face
And pleasant words in every place.
I pray, whatever wrong I do,
I may not say what is not true;
Be willing in my task each day,
And always honest in my play.
Make me unselfish with my joys,
And share with other girls and boys;
Kind and helpful to the old
And prompt to do what I am told.
Bless every one that I love, and teach
Me how to help and comfort each.
Give me the strength right living brings,
And make me good in little things. Amen.

Cradle Hymn

Away in a manger, no crib for a bed,
The little Lord Jesus laid down his sweet
head.
The stars in the bright sky looked down
where
he lay—
The little Lord Jesus asleep on the hay.

The cattle are lowing, the baby awakes,
But little Lord Jesus no crying he makes.
I love thee, Lord Jesus! Look down
from the sky,
And stay by my cradle till morning is nigh.

Be near me, Lord Jesus, I ask thee to stay
Close by me forever, and love me, I pray.
Bless all the dear children, in thy tender
care,
And take us to heaven, to live with thee
there.

Prayers on Entering and Leaving Church

Heavenly Father, this is your house. Help me to be sure that you are here and near to me. I cannot see you, but I feel your presence. I bow down my head and hush all my thoughts about other things in order that I may know you. Help me to express my thanks and to praise you; teach me what is best for me to know; help me to decide to do your will. Amen.

Dear Lord, I am your little child. Help me to sit quietly, to listen carefully and understand the meaning of all that is done in church today.

Dear Lord, as we leave church today help
me to remember the lessons I have heard.
Amen.

A Prayer Before Worship

Dear Father God, this is thy house,
   A lovely place to be;
We bow our heads, and close our eyes
   And learn to worship thee.

Richard H. Bennett

Giving

We like to give to those we love,
  And so we bring to thee
Our precious gifts, and leave them here,
  Dear Lord, for you to see.

Richard H. Bennett

A Prayer Before Singing

Dear Father, listen while we sing
    Our happy song to you;
It tells you that we love you,
    And we know you love us, too.

Richard H. Bennett

A Prayer Before Reading the Bible

And now we take your holy book,
    The Bible, in our hand;
We listen for your word to us,
    And try to understand.

Richard H. Bennett

Good-bye Prayer

We do not say good-bye to you,
 Dear God, for every day
You go with us and stay with us,
 At home, at school, at play.

Richard H. Bennett

I Would Be True

I would be true, for there are those who
   trust me;
I would be pure, for there are those who
   care;
I would be strong, for there is much to suffer;
I would be brave, for there is much to dare.
I would be friend of all—the foe, the
   friendless;
I would be giving, and forget the gift;
I would be humble, for I know my weakness;
I would look up, and laugh, and love, and
   lift.

Howard Arnold Walter

Savior, Teach Me, Day by Day

Savior, teach me, day by day,
Love's sweet lesson to obey;
Sweeter lesson cannot be,
Loving him who first loved me.

With a child-like heart of love,
At your bidding may I move;
Prompt to serve and follow thee,
Loving him who first loved me.

Teach me all your steps to trace,
Strong to follow in your grace,
Learning how to love from thee,
Loving him who first loved me.

Thus may I rejoice to show
That I feel the love I owe;
Singing, till your face I see,
Of his love who first loved me.

Jane E. Leeson, 1842

Some Scriptures to Make Your Own

Welcome Little Children

People were bringing little children to him in order that he might touch them; and the disciples spoke sternly to them. But when Jesus saw this, he was indignant and said to them, "Let the little children come to me; do not stop them; for it is to such that the kingdom of God belongs. Truly I tell you, whoever does not receive the kingdom of God as a little child will never enter it." And he took them up in his arms, laid his hands on them, and blessed them.

Mark 10:13-16

The Two Great Commandments

You shall love the Lord your God with all your heart, and with all your soul, and with all your mind. This is the greatest and first commandment. And a second is like it: "You shall love your neighbor as yourself."

Matthew 22:37-39

The Golden Rule

"In everything do to others as you would have them do to you."

Matthew 7:12

The Shema

Hear, O Israel: The Lord is our God, the Lord alone. You shall love the Lord your God with all your heart, and with all your soul, and with all your might.

Deuteronomy 6:4-5

Even Children

Even children make themselves
   known by their acts,
by whether what they do is
   pure and right.

Proverbs 20:11

The Twenty-third Psalm

The Lord is my shepherd; I shall not
  want.
He maketh me to lie down in green
  pastures:
He leadeth me beside still waters.
He restoreth my soul: he leadeth me in
  the paths of righteousness for his
  name's sake.
Yeah, though I walk through the valley of
  the shadow of death, I will fear no
  evil:
For thou art with me; thy rod and thy
  staff they comfort me.
Thou preparest a table before me in the
  presence of mine enemies:
Thou anointest my head with oil;
My cup runneth over.
Surely goodness and mercy shall follow
  me all the days of my life:
And I will dwell in the house of the Lord
  forever.

KJV

Psalm 100

Make a joyful noise to the Lord,
　　all the earth.
Worship the Lord with
　　gladness;
come into his presence with
　　singing.

Know that the Lord is God.
　　It is he that made us, and we
　　　　are his;
　　we are his people, and the
　　　　sheep of his pasture.

Enter his gates with
　　　　thanksgiving,
　　and his courts with praise.
　　Give thanks to him, bless his
　　　　name.

For the Lord is good;
    his steadfast love endures
        forever,
    and his faithfulness to all
        generations.

The Christmas Story

In those days a decree went out from Emperor Augustus that all the world should be registered. Joseph . . . went . . . to Bethlehem . . . to be registered with Mary, to whom he was engaged and who was expecting a child. While they were there, the time came for her to deliver her child. And she gave birth to her firstborn son and wrapped him in bands of cloth, and laid him in a manger, because there was no place for them in the inn.

In that region there were shepherds living in the fields, keeping watch over their flock by night. Then an angel of the Lord stood before them, and the glory of the Lord shone around them, and they were terrified. But the angel said to them, "Do not be afraid; for see—I am bringing you good news of great joy for all the people: to you is born this day in the city of David a

Savior, who is the Messiah, the Lord. This will be a sign for you: you will find a child wrapped in bands of cloth and lying in a manger. And suddenly there was with the angel a multitude of the heavenly host, praising God and saying,

"Glory to God in the highest heaven, and on earth peace among those whom he favors!"

When the angels had left them and gone into heaven, the shepherds said to one another, "Let us go now to Bethlehem and see this thing that has taken place, which the Lord has made known to us." So they went with haste and found Mary and Joseph, and the child lying in the manger.

Luke 2:1, 4-16